setting the course FOR FUTURE GENERATIONS

SHANE L. HUSEBY

SETTING THE COURSE FOR FUTURE GENERATIONS

by Shane L. Huseby

ISBN-13: 978-1-60273-024-3

ISBN-10: 1-60273-024-5

Library of Congress Control Number: 2012920635

Printed in the United States of America.

For World-Wide Distribution.

Front cover Art by Micah Gay.

Parsons Publishing House

P. O. Box 488

Stafford, VA 22554 USA

www.ParsonsPublishingHouse.com

Info@ParsonsPublishingHouse.com

TABLE OF CONTENTS

DEDICATION

This book is dedicated to my family: my wife, Julia–the woman of my dreams–and my two wonderful children, Anna and Sophia.

Julia: Your constant support and love have encouraged me to get out of my comfort zone and be who God has called me to be. Thank you for encouraging and believing in me. Life with you has truly been great.

Anna and Sophia: I am so proud of you and excited to see all the things God has in store for the two of you. God has a great destiny for each of you, and I am confident that as you seek the Lord with all your heart, His face will shine down upon you.

I would also like to express my love and appreciation for my grandparents and parents for establishing the foundation of faith that God has been able to build upon.

Finally, I want to express my deep, heartfelt love and appreciation to my pastors, Robert and Stacey Gay. Your love, wisdom, vision, and encouragement mean more to me than you will ever know. Thank you for expecting greater from me than I expected of myself. Thank you for being an anchor even in the midst of a storm and for facing the giants so I wouldn't have to.

FOREWORD

It is important that we have an understanding that God is interested in our families. Since the dawn of creation, God has always been a God of families. After creating Adam He said, "It is not good for man to be alone." He then created Eve to be a helper for the man and commissioned them to replenish the earth. In other words, God told them to have a family and reproduce another generation.

God revealed Himself in the Old Testament as the God of Abraham, Isaac, and Jacob. In doing so He declared that He is a God of generations. He is not merely interested in you, but your future generations. It has always been the plan of God that generations serve Him together. God's plan from the beginning was for man to reproduce and raise their families to serve the Lord together. We read in the Bible that Abraham commanded his children and God blessed him as a result. The blessing of Abraham is the result of a man God found that connected with the heart of the Father and allowed it to be demonstrated in his own family.

We see another demonstration of this principle in the institution of the tabernacle of David. There were three primary chief musicians: Asaph, Heman, and Jeduthun. These men functioned along with their sons in the arena of worship, praise, and the prophetic ministry in the house of the Lord. The fathers were not there by themselves. Their sons stood with them as they ministered together. In the New Testament, we then see how God is restoring the tabernacle of David. Part of that restoration involves generations serving the Lord and ministering together.

God loved us so much that He sent His only Son Jesus so that we would be a part of His family. We were estranged and separated from the Father because of sin. So Jesus came to purchase us with His own blood and in being raised from the dead He became the "first-born of many brethren." God's plan of salvation was all about family and generations. We are now the SONS of God; we are not servants, but SONS.

My wonderful wife, Stacey, and I have been married for 30 years and have three children. When they were growing up, we would travel together and they would minister by our side. This was a part of their training for that which God would later release in their lives. Today they are all serving the Lord and actively involved in full-time ministry.

Some have criticized family ministries. The reality is that it was the dream of God from the beginning. It has always been God's plan, and the devil hates it. That is part of the reason for the war on the family that is presently going on in our culture and society. The enemy hates the seed of the righteous and knows that dividing generations limits our effectiveness in the body of Christ. I have said for years that it will require more than one generation to fulfill the plan and purpose of God. It will require GENERATIONS walking together in a united manner.

Unfortunately, selfishness has affected many believers today. As a result, they have sacrificed their children on the altar of their own desires, whims, and personal dreams. To live without an understanding of the importance of family and future generations is the epitome of missing the heart of the Father God. It has been repeatedly demonstrated throughout the Bible that God is a God of generations.

God said through the prophet Malachi that His desire was that the hearts of the fathers be turned to the children and the children to the fathers. Failure of this would result in the manifestation of the curse. We can see that God takes this very seriously. Many of the problems that we have in our society today are the result of absentee fathers and mothers. "Latch-key kids" have become the norm as many children have no supervision, training, or accountability from their parents. The Word of God tells us that a child left to his own will bring his parents shame. This is disastrous and something must be done.

The solution is found in the principles of God's Word as it relates to families and generations. Shane Huseby expounds wonderfully on this all important topic that will bring revelation and understanding in your life. In this book ***Setting the Course for Future Generations***, Shane shares a Biblical perspective of the importance of family and future generations.

I have personally known the author for over ten years and can testify that He doesn't just talk the talk, but he walks the walk. He and his lovely wife Julia are a testament of a godly marriage and home with children being raised to serve the Lord. This book is sure to be a blessing to you and enlighten you to God's plan for you, your family, and future generations.

Pastor Robert Gay
High Praise Worship Center
Panama City, Florida USA

INTRODUCTION

It is no longer good enough for Christians to bring their children to church and expect that they will be productive citizens in the Kingdom of God. When my first child was born a weightiness of responsibility came down upon me that I was going to be held responsible for not only the well-being of my children, but also their spiritual well-being.

The strategies of satan are being unmasked, and the church is about to embark on the greatest season it has ever seen. This is a no-nonsense book–not for the faint-of-heart; but, I believe that the world is tired of fake Christianity and is ready for a realness that has been absent from many Christian homes.

Laziness dominates some Christian parents, thinking that having our children in church is good enough; they think they can leave the teaching of the things of God to their pastor or Sunday school teacher. All the while over ninety percent of our youth never return to the church once they graduate high school.

The purpose of this book is two-fold. First, I want to leave a spiritual inheritance to my children so that they may know that they are a small part of a big picture and that God isn't just interested in them, but He is a God of generations. Secondly, I want to amplify these truths to the Body of Christ so that fathers, mothers, and others are in one accord regarding God's generational yearnings. If Christians take hold of these truths and run with them, there will be a revolution in families, churches, and ultimately our nation.

CHAPTER ONE

GOD IS A GOD OF GENERATIONS

> *And he will turn the hearts of the fathers to the children, And the hearts of the children to their fathers, Lest I come and strike the earth with a curse* (Mal 4:6).

The day is here that God is bringing change in the hearts of His people to bring forth a restoration in each generation, old and young alike, walking hand-in-hand to establish His Kingdom in the earth. God is revealing Himself to His people as a God of generations.

"I am the God of your father–the God of Abraham, the God of Isaac, and the God of Jacob" (Ex 3:6 NIV).

By not only declaring that He is the God of Abraham, but also of Isaac and Jacob, God is making a declaration of His character and His nature, that He is concerned about generations and that He thinks generationally.

> *"'After this I will return and will rebuild the tabernacle of David, which has fallen down; I will rebuild its ruins, and I will set it up; So that the rest of mankind may seek the LORD, Even all the Gentiles who are called by My name, says the LORD who does all these things'"* (Acts 15:16-17).

Here we see that the Lord declared that there will be a day–which I believe is today–that He will restore the tabernacle of David. In the tabernacle, there was praise and worship of God twenty-four hours a day, seven days a week. The tabernacle of David, being defined not as an actual tent being placed upon mount Zion once again, but as a restoration of praise and worship and also a restoration of fatherhood ministry and generations working together to do God's will in the earth. We must understand the need for being true fathers with the Father's heart. True fathers will take responsibility when others will not. Fathers will require of their children; they will hold a high expectation for them. I believe that the greatest disservice a father can do to his children is to hold a low expectation for his child. We must train our children to be the best that they can be.

In the quote above, Peter states what is revealed in the Old Testament in Amos chapter nine, "On that day I will raise up The tabernacle of David, which has fallen down, And repair its damages; I will raise up its ruins..." (Amos 9:11).

We must understand that the restoration of the tabernacle of David is not just a restoration of praise and worship, but also a restoration of generations serving God together.

I believe that God wants to **restore** to His people the way we think about the generations in our families that are yet to come. We are not just to think about our own well-being and spiritual condition, but the condition of future generations into which we have imparted values and beliefs. We have a responsibility to pass certain things on from one generation to another. I use the word "restore" because this is not a new concept, but an example that we see in the Word of God.

We see people of God instill, train, and mentor future generations and pass on a lineage of fruitful, godly people. On the other hand, we also see people of God that do not instill, train, or mentor upcoming generations and it leads to a lineage of ungodly, rebellious, people. For people who have taken the things of God seriously, we see great fruit. An example of this can be found in 1 Chronicles 25:1-8:

> *Moreover David and the captains of the army separated for the service*

some of ***the sons*** *of Asaph, of Heman, and of Jeduthun, who should prophesy with harps, stringed instruments, and cymbals. And the number of the skilled men performing their service was: Of* ***the sons*** *of Asaph: Zaccur, Joseph, Nethaniah, and Asharelah;* ***the sons*** *of Asaph were* ***under the direction of Asaph,*** *who prophesied according to the order of the king. Of Jeduthun,* ***the sons*** *of Jeduthun: Gedaliah, Zeri, Jeshaiah, Shimei, Hashabiah, and Mattithiah, six,* ***under the direction of their father*** *Jeduthun, who prophesied with a harp to give thanks and to praise the LORD. Of Heman, the sons of Heman: Bukkiah, Mattaniah, Uzziel, Shebuel, Jerimoth, Hananiah, Hanani, Eliathah, Giddalti, Romamti-Ezer, Joshbekashah, Mallothi, Hothir, and Mahazioth. All these were* ***the sons*** *of Heman the king's seer in the words of God, to exalt his horn. For God gave Heman* ***fourteen sons and three daughters.*** *All these were* ***under the direction of their father*** *for the music in the house of the LORD, with cymbals, stringed instruments, and harps, for the service of the house of God. Asaph, Jeduthun, and Heman were under the authority of the king. So the number of them, with* ***their brethren*** *who were instructed in the*

> *songs of the LORD, all who were skillful, was two hundred and eighty-eight. And they cast lots for their duty, the small as well as the great,* ***the teacher with the student*** (1 Chr 25:1-8, emphasis added).

What we see in this Scripture is that Asaph, Heman, and Jeduthun not only served in the tabernacle, but their sons also served. In verse six when it says "all these," it is referring not only to their sons, but to their daughters, as well. Here we have fathers reproducing themselves in their children or raising and training their children to serve God; we could even say they were involved in family ministry. The pattern we see in God's Word is sons and daughters standing by their fathers and learning the things of the Lord. We also see that the children were skillful in their tasks. Not only were they skillful in the things of the Lord, but they ministered with their fathers side-by-side. This is an example of what God blesses and in what He takes great delight.

It is time that fathers step up to the plate and be the man God has called them to be. As fathers, we all have the responsibility to mentor and train our children. In this day and age, our society is filled with children who have no fathers. Mothers are doing their best to fill a gap that they should not have to fill. This is certainly not God's best for children. However, there are pastors and godly men out there who can be an example to those children. God brought Elijah as a mentor to Elisha, and as a result, Elisha left with a double portion of God's anointing.

What you have to understand is that your child is also the Lord's child for whom He has a great destiny. Knowing that brings a great sense of responsibility in the importance of the way we raise our children. A child with the seed of the Lord within them should be at the top of their class, well-behaved, have the peace of the Lord, and have confidence to do well in life. I say these things based on what God's Word says about the way all of His people should live their lives.

"I can do all things through Christ who strengthens me" (Phil 4:13).

> *And the LORD will make you the head and not the tail; you shall be above only, and not be beneath, if you heed the commandments of the LORD your God, which I command you today, and are careful to observe them* (Deut 28:13).

"Train up a child in the way he should go, And when he is old he will not depart from it" (Prov 22:6).

What we have seen in the past is great men and women of God who have children that serve the devil, and in the words of the Apostle James, "My brethren, these things ought not to be!" It is amazing how Christian parents will train and make their children brush their teeth, take a bath, and even go to school, but put little or no emphasis on the things of God. I have also seen children trained in the things of God at an early age, but when they get a little older the importance of God's Kingdom is lost.

In the past, we have seen families whose children are not trained in the way they should be, in fact, a lot of parents make training their children the responsibility of the day care or school system. Today we see many children going to day care, and by no means am I criticizing parents for having to use day care services because in this day and age parents sometimes have to work hours that prevent them from keeping their own children. However, I have seen and heard of even Christian parents leaving their children in a day care just because they do not want to "deal" with their children. I have heard parents say, "I am just not the fatherly or motherly type." This is a sad attitude to have for a parent. Instead of having someone else raising your child and imparting to them their views, whether good or bad, parents should be the ones doing the imparting and taking a proactive role in the lives of their children.

Because you had children, you are now responsible to God to raise them up in a godly fashion. Parents are primarily responsible to train up their children the right way, not to have some government program or organization raise their child with their secular humanistic views when the parents are well-able to train them. What we have seen is that when these children get older and leave home, the things of God do not have an importance in their lives. I say this because Proverbs 22:6 says that if we train our children the right way (the way he should go) he will not depart from it. In other words, the things of God are of such importance to our children they will continue in the ways of the Lord.

Now, please understand my heart, by no means am I condemning anyone if their children have fallen by the wayside because we are all human, and we all make mistakes. That being said, it does not matter what has happened in the past. The past is the past and we can do things differently from this day forward. Thankfully, God is a God of restoration and He can bring the prodigal sons and daughters home once again and redeem the time that has been lost. Oh hallelujah, our God is an awesome God!

As Christian parents, especially fathers, we need to see the pattern God sets before us in His Word to train the future scientists, presidents, judges, lawmakers, attorneys, business people, firefighters, nurses, doctors, police officers, military personnel, and ministers of His Word.

CHAPTER TWO

PASSING THE TORCH

The desire to separate generations is from our enemy. There should never be a division between generations, but a passing of the torch from one generation to another in order to work together for the establishing of God's Kingdom. As my children are growing up, I have a commission and a responsibility to pass on to them the revelation and knowledge God has given me in order to be a platform for them to go higher and farther than I ever will. Just as Paul encouraged Timothy to stir up the gift of God that was passed down to him through the laying on of Paul's hands, Timothy went on to be a great minister of the gospel.

"Therefore, I remind you to stir up the gift of God which is in you through the laying on of my hands" (2 Tim 1:6).

In this next passage of Scripture, Paul bases his urgent appeal on the reality of his imminent death. In light of the contemporary situation, we see Timothy's responsibility was to be faithful in fulfilling his ministry:

> *For I am already being poured out as a drink offering, and the time of my departure is at hand. I have fought the good fight, I have finished the race, I have kept the faith. Finally, there is laid up for me the crown of righteousness, which the Lord, the righteous Judge, will give to me on that Day, and not to me only but also to all who have loved His appearing* (2 Tim 4:6-8).

Generations serving God together cause great damage to the kingdom of hell. In order to try to minimize the damage God's people cause in satan's kingdom, the enemy tries to bring division between the generations. One way the enemy does this is by selling the lie that children have to go sow their wild oats. This is a lie from the innermost parts of hell, and we should never entertain these thoughts. It amazes me how easily many Christian parents fall for this lie. Our children do not have to be exposed to the garbage the enemy lays out before them. It is our job as parents who stand for righteousness, to protect the hearts and minds of our children. Do not be ignorant of satan's devices, but be on guard; be vigilant for the protection of our children.

"My people are destroyed for lack of knowledge" (Hos 4:6).

The first chapter of Job is an example of how we should pray and intercede for our children daily. I know that my natural father prays and intercedes for all of his children. Because of this, I believe that we have been saved from a lot of heartache and trouble because a hedge of protection has been placed around about us by his intercession. I am not saying we haven't had our share of trials, but I know that they could have been a lot worse if it had not been for the prayers of our father and mother. By doing so, we empower our children to do great things. Today I am able to do things that my father was not able to do at my age; I have been able to build upon the foundation he imparted to me.

The enemy strives to stop this from happening so he seeks to devour each generation in order to prevent God's reproductive anointing from taking place in family lineage. Satan, not being able to do anything new but only pervert what God has created, does the same thing repeatedly, so when we see him rise up his old ugly face we can put a stop to it in the name of Jesus. Nevertheless, I am declaring to you today that God's Word will prevail and the kingdoms of this world will become the kingdoms of our God.

> *This charge I commit to you, son Timothy, according to the prophecies previously made concerning you, that by them you may wage the good warfare* (1 Tim 1:18).

We must be true fathers with the Father's heart to reproduce ourselves, in not only our natural children, but in others as well. You don't have to have natural children in order to be a father figure, mentor, or to be a blessing to younger generations whether they are your relatives or not. God can use you because you have something to offer. Whether you realize it or not, God has placed giftings, talents, and anointings in all of His people. So yes, even you have something to offer! In 1 Timothy 1:18 quoted earlier, Paul refers to Timothy as "son." Even though Timothy was not Paul's natural son, Paul mentored and trained him to carry on after he was gone. Because of this, Timothy went on to do great and mighty miracles and exploits for the Kingdom of God.

We must understand that the balance to this is that no one can take the place of someone's natural father, but that does not mean you can't mentor others, like Paul was there for Timothy.

One example we see today is the office of the pastor that functions and operates in this fatherly role. In fact, we can see godly examples of fathers all throughout the Word, Jesus being the ultimate example.

As we pass the torch from one generation to another we must be willing to stay the course, no matter if it harelips the devil or anyone else. Fathers blaze the trail so that their children will not have to.

My wife and I have had to face issues that the enemy set up which were designed to prevent us from fulfilling our destiny. By facing these giants and putting the enemy under our feet, our children will not have to face the same giants, but go on to fulfill God's destiny that He has for them. We must be willing to say the buck stops here and commit to do what previous generations refused to do in order to overcome the giants in the land or longstanding family issues. God wants to revolutionize the way we think about upcoming generations, and when His people get hold of this truth it will take the world by storm. This will not just be a revival, but a revolution.

"He who spares his rod hates his son, but he who loves him disciplines him promptly" (Prov 13:24).

As fathers, we should reprove and rebuke our children. It is ridiculous in this day and age that humanistic teaching has infiltrated the Christian home and has told parents that by disciplining their children they would crush or damage their spirit; this is nothing but hogwash. By not disciplining our children, we allow them to grow up to be nonproductive, spoiled, egotistical grownups that have no respect for authority. We must again approach every area of our lives according to the Word of God which covers every situation that we may face, including the discipline of our children.

"Let all things be done decently and in order" (1 Cor 14:40).

Fathers do not negotiate or compromise, but lead by reinforcing values within their children and teaching them to live righteously. Fathers will love their children, spend time with their children, and even when necessary bring discipline and order into their children's lives. I am embarrassed to say that I have seen Christian fathers who do not even care to spend time with their children, much less teach them about the things of God. This should not be. Parents must not be selfish when it comes to their children. There is great responsibility that God's people dismiss in the raising up of future generations. Parents must make time to train their children because, after all, our children are our heritage.

"For the Lord disciplines him whom he loves, and chastises every son whom he receives" (Heb 12:6 RSV).

CHAPTER THREE

GOD IS INTERESTED IN YOUR FAMILY

> *Our Father in heaven, hallowed be your name, your kingdom come, your will be done on earth as it is in heaven* (Matt 6:9-10).

Contrary to the belief of some, our families and this world do not belong to satan, but to the Lord. God is interested in, not only what happens on the earth, but also what takes place within our family lines. We must have a vision of what God wants our children to accomplish and impart that vision to our children. Some have asked, "How do I know what God is saying?" First, we should know that God is always saying something and just like listening to a radio, we have to tune ourselves in with God to the right frequency.

"My sheep hear My voice, and I know them, and they follow Me" (John 10:27).

In the natural, my grandfathers left a physical inheritance for my parents that will one day be passed down to my siblings and myself, that will also be passed down to our children. Today in the spiritual realm, I see that through past generations in our family God has imparted certain truths and revelations to my grandparents and parents, which they have imparted to me. In turn, I will also pass them down to my children and so forth. What God imparts to us should be a foundation for the truth and revelation He gives our children. God builds upon the revelations of past generations to fulfill His Word and to establish His Kingdom in the hearts and minds of future generations.

"The earth is the Lord's, and everything in it, the world, and all who live in it" (Ps 24:1 NIV).

As God's people, we should look past today and into tomorrow. We must look ahead to the generations in our family that have not even been born yet. It has never been God's will for generations to be separated, but to pass along a spiritual inheritance from one generation to another for the establishing of God's kingdom.

Just like in the days of old, today we see generations serving God together. We see Abraham, Isaac, and Jacob, Asaph and sons, Heman and sons, Jeduthun and sons, and David and Solomon. We also see more recent generations serving side by side like Kenneth Hagin, Kenneth Hagin Jr., and Craig Hagin, Billy and Franklin Graham, Oral and Richard Roberts, Kenneth Copeland and his children. This is the example we are to follow.

The best thing for our children is to serve God. When God's people really serve Him and do His bidding instead of just being in the Kingdom for fire insurance, life has a fulfillment that others might not understand. When you are serving God and training your children to do the same there is a peace and an anticipation of what God will do through you and your children even in the midst of opposition.

Sometimes God calls you to do things that are not easy. Others, even friends and family might oppose you, but God never told us it would be easy. In fact, Jesus even said, "In the world there will be trials and tribulation but be of good cheer for I have overcome the world." Through God we can do anything, no matter what opposes us in the midst of doing God's will; after all God's Word tells us that we can do all things through Christ Jesus who strengthens us.

"Therefore submit to God. Resist the devil and he will flee from you" (James 4:7).

We must reproduce in our children godly principles that will cause them to be men and women of integrity in the days ahead. We should teach children not just to be a Christian and to love God, but to live their lives according to the Word of God in every area, constantly seeking His purpose and will every day. Instead of the enemy destroying our families and taking our children, I see more and more generational service in God's army.

Looking back in the natural, there have been generations within my own family that have fought, bled, and even died, in just about every major campaign this great country has faced in order to resist an aggressor to maintain the liberties and freedoms that we enjoy and cherish every day. My friend you have to know that when you become a Christian you just enlisted into the army of God and there is a war that has been raging through the ages against an aggressor that is trying to take away what is rightfully ours and bring bondage and slavery to God's people. We must stand fast and not desert our post because the final outcome of this war that we face has already been determined: we are the winner if we fight and do not give up.

> *But if serving the LORD seems undesirable to you, then choose for yourselves this day whom you will serve, whether the gods your forefathers served beyond the River, or the gods of the Amorites, in whose land you are living. But as for me and my*

> *household, we will serve the LORD* (Josh 24:15 NIV).

As Christians, we must choose whom we and our families will serve. We can serve either the devil or God, but not both. Serving God is not about a fad or a nice thing to do, but serving Him and training our children to do so is the least we can do for all that He has done for us. I know many Christians, even family members, who seem like *they could* take or leave what God has for them because of disappointments of the past, hurts, or a perverted or distorted view of who God really is. One reason many Christians feel this way and even leave God's church looking for something else is because they don't know who God really is. This can be discovered through the studying of God's Word, prayer, and meditating on Him.

In these days and in the days ahead, riding the fence will not cut it any longer, but will only expose you to the enemy for your very own demise. Living a lukewarm, mediocre life is not good enough anymore. We have to pursue the things of God with everything that is within us. We see biblical patterns of families serving God and those who do not. For families who serve God together, we see generational blessings, and for those who do not, generational curses.

Men have the responsibility to set the pattern in their families for generational service to God, not sit on the couch reading the Sunday paper while their wife takes the children to church. As the head of my home, I must lead by example, not being a hypocrite by saying one thing and my children seeing me do something else. Men have to assume their godly role in their family. This role that I speak of is not one of a tyrant who rules with an iron fist, but one of a loving, caring parent who will also bring order and correction when needed.

> *I know your deeds, that you are neither cold nor hot. I wish you were either one or the other! So, because you are lukewarm–neither hot nor cold–I am about to spit you out of my mouth* (Rev 3:15-16 NIV).

The biblical pattern that we see in the Word is one of success in accomplishing God's will. We see that when God's people follow His pattern they are successful in the work they do for the Kingdom. Through Abraham, we see generational blessings passed on to Isaac and Jacob and even on down to God's people today. Just like with Abraham, God brought blessings upon families like those of Asaph, Heman, and Jeduthun for reproducing themselves into the lives of their children.

Generational blessings are just a byproduct of training your children and other generations for the service of the Kingdom of

God. There are also generational curses that come upon families as a result of disobedience and not training the upcoming generations to serve God. If God's people will not take responsibility to train upcoming generations in the importance of the things of God, then their children will not know the blessings that God has for them. Furthermore, generation upon generation will keep going around the same old mountain never fulfilling their destiny and never receiving the inheritance that is rightfully theirs. God does not suggest, but requires, us to be obedient to Him, and if we are not we will end up just like the children of Israel that never entered into their promised land.

> *For I, the LORD your God, am a jealous God, visiting the iniquity of the fathers upon the children to the third and fourth generations of those who hate Me, but showing mercy to thousands, to those who love Me and keep My commandments* (Deut 5:9-10).

Many individuals and families are called for generational service for the Kingdom of God, and I am not just talking about service in ministry as we discussed earlier, but also a willingness to do all that God has called you to do. I would go as far to say that most Christians never accomplish all things that God has for them. I once heard a saying that graveyards are the richest places in the world because of talents and anointings that never were tapped into for one reason or another. Because of this, books and songs were never written and patents and ideas never pursued.

"For many are called, but few chosen" (Matt 20:16).

God has given us an opportunity to do His will in the earth, so do not be like others and not take responsibility to answer that call. We must not have a wilderness mentality, wanting everything and doing nothing.

> *After the death of Moses the servant of the LORD, it came to pass that the LORD spoke to Joshua the son of Nun, Moses' assistant, saying: "Moses My servant is dead. Now therefore, arise, go over this Jordan, you and all this people, to the land which I am giving to them–the children of Israel. Every place that the sole of your foot will tread upon I have given you, as I said to Moses"* (Josh 1:1-3).

Here we see a biblical example of generational service. God tells Joshua that he is to take the place of Moses and lead his people into the Promised Land. All along, Moses was reproducing himself in Joshua to accomplish God's will. This was a great responsibility for Joshua.

As we go forth to take hold of our inheritance as Joshua did, we must also take our responsibility seriously and refuse to let discouragement come in or be swayed by the opinions of man. I never said that doing God's will is always easy. Joshua and the children of Israel had to take their inheritance by force, which is exactly what we may have to do. However, do not be discouraged for in the end it will all be worth it.

CHAPTER FOUR

GOD IS ILLUMINATING GENERATIONAL UNDERSTANDING IN HIS PEOPLE

Some think that in order to do God's will and work they have to be in full-time ministry. This, however, is not true. God's people can do His work and bidding in every area whether it be in the political realm, business realm, entertainment realm, or any other area of today's society. The Word is full of examples of mighty ministers that God used to do great and mighty things. These people were not in full-time ministry, but did God's will where they worked and lived which ended up bringing life, freedom, liberty, and breakthrough to many people.

We must stop being lazy and quit expecting our local ministers to do all the work. God has called all of His people to do His work. We can witness, minister, be an example, and stand for what is right in whatever area of society we live and work.

> *For though by this time you ought to be teachers, you need someone to teach you again the first principles of the oracles of God; and you have come to need milk and not solid food. For everyone who partakes only of milk is unskilled in the word of righteousness, for he is a babe. But solid food belongs to those who are of full age, that is, those who by reason of use have their senses exercised to discern both good and evil* (Heb 5:12-14).

Many believers think that the main purpose for ministers and the church is to get people saved, instead of them having their own part to play in doing God's work. In fact, I have been in many churches while growing up where all you hear in every service is a salvation message. Consequently, you have a church full of spiritual babies because they do not know about anything else but being saved, and they are all already saved. That being the case, the church is no mighty army breaking down the strongholds of hell, but is nothing more than a spiritual daycare. This is one thing that plagues the church today.

Please understand how I say this. While the salvation message is good and necessary, not as many people get saved in church compared to the amount that could be saved out in society if God's people would go out into their work and every area of society and spread the Good News. The salvation message is a necessary part of our Christian walk; however, if that is all you hear you remain immature in your walk with God. Salvation is the beginning of our victorious walk with Christ, but you do not continue in your spiritual growth on the salvation message alone–you only learn how to be saved again. Therefore, people are not equipped as they should be to do God's work of getting people saved and bringing them to church. Some people think that doing God's work is the job of the full-time minister only, but the people of God must instead continue to grow by hearing about the fullness of God and their responsibilities and duties as ambassadors of Christ. Instead of hearing about only one aspect of God, let us not stay babies drinking only milk, but grow up eating the meat of the Word of God so that we can be instruments of His righteousness in the earth.

> *And I, brethren, could not speak to you as to spiritual people but as to carnal, as to babes in Christ. I fed you with milk and not with solid food; for until now you were not able to receive it, and even now you are still not able; for you are still carnal. For where there are envy, strife, and divisions among you, are you not carnal and behaving like mere men?* (1 Cor 3:1-3).

In Deuteronomy six, we see how God puts importance on passing anointing, revelation, and knowledge of His Kingdom to the younger generations.

> *"The Lord your God told me to give you all these commandments which you are to obey in the land you will soon be entering, where you will live. The purpose of these laws is to cause you, your sons, and your grandsons to reverence the Lord your God by obeying all of his instructions as long as you live; if you do, you will have long, prosperous years ahead of you"* (Deut 6:1-2 TLB).

God means what He says and says what He means. When God tells us to do something it is only for our best interest because He sees the big picture. Yes, God gives us a free will and we have a choice whether we obey him or not; however, God's commands are exactly that, commands not suggestions.

I hear people say all the time, "This thing happened to me" or "that happened to me" or even, "God is doing this horrible or bad thing to me." The fact of the matter is most of the time when you look at their situation the reason that things aren't going well with them is because of their own disobedience which is referenced in Deuteronomy twenty eight verse fifteen, because they are not obeying all of God's commandments. I am not saying that as we are obedient we will never go through anything bad or negative. However, if we do go through something like that, there is a peace and grace that gets us through. Jesus said that in this world we would have trials and tribulation, but that we should be of good cheer for He has already overcome the world. Deuteronomy six affirms to us that as we live an obedient lifestyle God will bless us and our generations, with long and prosperous lives.

> *"Therefore, O Israel, listen closely to each command and be careful to obey it, so that all will go well with you, and so that you will have many children. If you obey these commands, you will become a great nation in a glorious land 'flowing with milk and honey,' even as the God of your fathers promised you"* (Deut 6:3 TLB).

As we obey God, He ushers us into our promised land. Many Christians think that our promises will just be dropped in our lap; I wish this were true. However, God takes us through a process most of the time. God gave the children of Israel their promised land flowing with milk and honey, but what we do not realize is that there were cows to milk, beehives to rob, and giants to slay. When we think about the Promised Land, we seem to think there were rivers of milk. We think that bees just had their honey ready in mason jars, and the giants and occupants of the land just handed the land over to Israel. However, this is not the case. God saw the big picture and took the nation of Israel through a process by which they had to occupy their land by force. Do not miss out on your promises, thinking they will just fall into your lap, but fight for them if necessary.

> *"O Israel, listen: Jehovah is our God, Jehovah alone. You must love him with all your heart, soul, and might. And you must think constantly about these commandments I am giving you today. You must teach them to your children and talk about them when you are at home or out for a walk; at bedtime and the first thing in the morning. Tie them on your finger, wear them on your forehead, and write them on the doorposts of your house!"* (Deut 6:4-9 TLB).

God stresses the importance of His Word to us; in fact, He says to constantly think about what His Word says and keep it in your heart. Deuteronomy six verse seven says it all: we are to constantly teach our children the things of God in every area of life, so when they are adults they will be prepared and able to accomplish anything God has for them. This should be done generation upon generation.

> *"When the Lord your God has brought you into the land he promised your ancestors, Abraham, Isaac, and Jacob, and when he has given you great cities full of good things-cities you didn't build, wells you didn't dig, and vineyards and olive trees you didn't plant-and when you have eaten until you can hold no more, then beware lest you forget the Lord who brought you out of the land of Egypt, the land of slavery. When you are full, don't forget to be reverent to him and to serve him and to use his name alone to endorse your promises"* (Deut 6:10-13 TLB).

We should never forget where God has brought us from, and in fact, we should share it with upcoming generations. I can remember both sets of my grandparents sharing stories of the great things God has done in their lives, and it has inspired me to trust God to do the same in my life. You see, God has many great and mighty things for us if we choose to serve Him and stake a claim on His promises to us.

> *"You must not worship the gods of the neighboring nations, for Jehovah your God who lives among you is a jealous God, and his anger may rise quickly against you, and wipe you off the face of the earth. You must not*

> *provoke him and try his patience as you did when you complained against him at Massah. You must actively obey him in everything he commands. Only then will you be doing what is right and good in the Lord's eyes. If you obey him, all will go well for you, and you will be able to go in and possess the good land that the Lord promised your ancestors. You will also be able to throw out all the enemies living in your land, as the Lord agreed to help you do*" (Deut 6:14-19 TLB).

A lot of Christians view God as a Santa Clause type character. They think that anything goes, and they really do not have to change their lifestyle and that God will just forgive them. Today's Christians have a "sloppy *agape*" mentality, and it seems like they have never read about God being a jealous God. Therefore, they live their lives in compromise, flirting with God's enemies. So the world looks at them thinking that there is nothing true or attractive about the Kingdom of God, and says Christians are nothing but a bunch of hypocrites. Christians cannot live flirting with a life of compromise and expect to be the bride of Christ. He is coming back for a pure and spotless bride, not one that has other lovers on the side, but a bride who only has a heart and eyes for Him.

> *"In the years to come when your son asks you, 'What is the purpose of these laws which the Lord our God has given us?' you must tell him, 'We were Pharaoh's slaves in Egypt, and the Lord brought us out of Egypt with great power and mighty miracles-with terrible blows against Egypt and Pharaoh and all his people. We saw it all with our own eyes. He brought us out of Egypt so that he could give us this land he had promised to our ancestors. And he has commanded us to obey all of these laws and to reverence him so that he can preserve us alive as he has until now. For it always goes well with us when we obey all the laws of the Lord our God'"* (Deut 6:20-25 TLB).

This passage of Scripture is a prime example of how God wants us to share His goodness with upcoming generations, as we are obedient to His Word. It is important that we never forget from where God has brought us. In fact, when I think about where He has taken me from and where He has taken me to, my faith arises and it is easier to trust Him no matter what giant I face. Just as David overcame when faced with Goliath, he remembered the victories that God had given him. When others even said that he could not do it David's response was, "Your servant has killed both lion and bear; and this uncircumcised Philistine will be like one of them, seeing he has defied the armies of the living God."

CHAPTER FIVE

IMPARTING GOD'S VISION TO OUR CHILDREN

We must impart God's vision to our children. God wants to impart some of the dreams and visions that you have to future generations.

> *"Now it was in the heart of my father David to build a temple for the name of the LORD God of Israel. But the LORD said to my father David, 'Whereas it was in your heart to build a temple for My name, you did well that it was in your heart. Nevertheless you shall not build the temple, but your son who will come from your body, he shall build the temple for My name.' So the LORD has fulfilled His word which He spoke; and I have filled the position of my father David, and sit on the throne of Israel, as the LORD promised; and I have built a temple*

> *for the name of the LORD God of Israel. And there I have made a place for the ark, in which is the covenant of the LORD which He made with our fathers, when He brought them out of the land of Egypt"* (1 Kings 8:17-21).

Here we see the vision God gave David that was passed down to Solomon, who took the vision and plan of God and ran with it. We must be willing, not only to impart the vision God has given us, but also to pass the baton to future generations and encourage them to step out and run with the vision. We can't, however, be so concerned about them making mistakes that we never let them step out; after all that is what training and nurturing younger generations is all about: letting them step out, allowing them to make a mistake without condemning them for it, and being there to pick them up if necessary.

To adults, riding a bicycle seems easy, but not to kids. In fact, it is very intimidating at first. You can sit your child down to watch a video about how to ride a bike and even read books to them on riding bikes, but they actually won't ever learn how to do it unless they get on a bicycle and try riding. In fact, when I was learning for the first time to ride I remember wrecking a lot. However, my parents were there to pick me up and encourage me to get back in the saddle, because quitting was not an option! It is funny when we look at our first bicycles to see they are all scratched up and the paint does not look as nice as it once did, but now we can ride without any help. The same goes for the generations ahead. Allow them to make mistakes, and if they do, be there to pick them up and encourage them not to quit.

Generations are needed to accomplish the purpose and plan of God. The vision in David's heart could not be fulfilled by himself. God placed a vision in David so he could impart a vision to generations ahead. Some of the visions, dreams, and revelations we have today have been given to us in order to impart to a generation still to come. Generations ahead need our visions and revelations as a foundation they can build upon in order to fulfill their destiny.

"Where there is no vision, the people perish: but he that keepeth the law, happy is he" (Prov 29:18 KJV).

Where there is no vision things are thrown into a chaotic state, but where there is vision there is order. The poorest person in the world is the person without a vision. When a person does not have a vision, life loses its meaning which leads to a lack of hope. Every day I go out into society I can tell the people that have no vision just by looking at them;

there is a look of hopelessness in their eyes. In fact, they look like they are just existing until they die. I know this sounds depressing, but it is the truth; far too many people live this way. God has created each of us in a specific and certain way, and not only that, He has given each of us a unique vision that we are to fulfill just like Solomon. When you fulfill your vision, it brings a purpose and a new meaning to your life. Far too many people go after the vision of others. God has not called us to copy someone else's purpose, but to find our own vision and destiny.

> *And said, "Men of Galilee, why are you standing here staring at the sky? Jesus has gone away to heaven, and some day, just as he went, he will return!"* (Acts 1:11 TLB).

The church has been crippled because of a lack of long-term vision. Much of the church has not been effective in the earth due to waiting for the rapture bus. Many Christians are just waiting for Jesus to come back, just like generations before waited for hundreds and even thousands of years. In Acts 1:11, angels came to the disciples and asked them why they were staring toward heaven instead of doing what Jesus told them to do which was to wait in Jerusalem until they were empowered after they received the Holy Spirit. Afterward, Jesus told them there was work to be done, and they would be His witnesses in Jerusalem, and in all of Judea and Samaria, and to the uttermost parts of the earth. The Word does say that Jesus will return one day; however, it also makes it clear that we are to go about establishing God's Kingdom in the earth until He does come back.

Most Christians who are waiting for the rapture bus are non-productive citizens in God's Kingdom. This is a main reason why the United States–a Christian nation founded by Christian men on Christian principles–has become what it is today. Since Christians have had their bags packed waiting to go to Heaven, ungodly people have infiltrated the government, school systems, entertainment arena, and every area of society. You see, we, as God's people, have handed over to the enemy the land that our God has called us to occupy. Since we have not occupied the land or certain sectors of society, the enemy has come in and perverted it. It is time to unpack our bags and take back what Satan has stolen! It is time to stop staring into the sky and allow God to restore His vision to us. As members of the Kingdom of God, we need to have His long-term vision so we can do His will, and so we can be used by Him to establish His Kingdom in the earth.

> *Then God blessed them, and God said to them, "Be fruitful and multiply; fill the earth and subdue it; have do-*

minion over the fish of the sea, over the birds of the air, and over every living thing that moves on the earth" (Gen 1:28).

CHAPTER SIX

GOD WANTS TO RESTORE GENERATIONAL MINISTRY & ANOINTING

"Train up a child in the way he should go, And when he is old he will not depart from it" (Prov 22:6).

When it comes to training our children, we have to realize it is probably one of the most important things in life that we can do. Many times I see parents being trained by their children, trying to negotiate with them for good behavior, instead of letting their "no" be "no" and their "yes" be "yes." The Word tells us in Proverbs 22:15 that foolishness is bound up in a child, and then it gives us God's way of dealing with our children's foolishness.

"Foolishness is bound up in the heart of a child; The rod of correction will drive it far from him" (Prov 22:15).

As a child, I thought that Proverbs 22:15 was my parent's favorite Scripture. However, as an adult I realize that by my parents disciplining me, and yes, even by using the gigantic rod of correction, my spirit was not crushed. I did not grow up with some complex as a result of getting my bottom spanked. Moreover, I will go so far as to say that it did not destroy my relationship with my parents. In fact, I look back and see that they had my best interest at heart; that being the case, they protected me from many things.

We see in the Word that God deals with us the way He wants us to deal with our children. In Hebrews 12:5-6, we see how God disciplines us as His children. Today we are in a society that says it is wrong to discipline your children. In fact, they say that you should never spank them in any way. Some say to give your child a countdown and hope they don't call your bluff because, after all, you might just have do something. My friends, this is a recipe for disaster in the home. Where there is no discipline you have spoiled brats for children who have no respect for rules. Furthermore, when they get older nothing changes, and they are still spoiled brats. We need to have a different mindset of God's discipline and know that discipline should not just be done out of love, but also that discipline should be done.

> *"My son, do not make light of the Lord's discipline, and do not lose heart when he rebukes you, because the Lord disciplines those he loves, and he punishes everyone he accepts as a son"* (Heb 12:5b-6 NIV).

> *Only be careful, and watch yourselves closely so that you do not forget the things your eyes have seen or let them slip from your heart as long as you live. Teach them to your children and to their children after them. Remember the day you stood before the LORD your God at Horeb, when he said to me, "Assemble the people before me to hear my words so that they may learn to revere me as long as they live in the land and may teach them to their children"* (Deut 4:9-10 NIV).

God tells us all through His Word to train our children in His ways. He does not limit our training material to what you might call traditional Bible stories like Jonah and the big fish, David and Goliath, and Daniel and the lion's den. We all know these wonderful stories and they are good to know, but there is so much more to the Kingdom of God than these great stories. The problem is a lot of adult Christians do not know much more than these stories. I know parents who are on fire for the Lord and they have even raised their children in church, but when the children get older they do not want to have anything to do with church or the things of God until they are in a mess.

When I was a youth pastor I saw this happen all the time. In fact, I still see this today. The problem is parents trust the church to train their children. It is not the church, the senior pastor's or the youth pastor's responsibility to instill the principles of God's Kingdom in their child's life, but it is the parent's responsibility first and foremost. In fact, parents who think that it's good enough to bring their children to church, and raise them in a Christian home, are sadly mistaken. This is a warped way to think since the only person God has ordained to train your child is you. Parents have to instill discipline in their child to carry out living a godly life. These things ought not to be!

> *"So keep these commandments carefully in mind. Tie them to your hand to remind you to obey them, and tie them to your forehead between your eyes! Teach them to your children. Talk about them when you are sitting at home, when you are out walking, at bedtime, and before breakfast! Write them upon the doors of your houses and upon your gates, so that as long*

> *as there is sky above the earth, you and your children will enjoy the good life awaiting you in the land the Lord has promised you"* (Deut 11:18-21 TLB).

We all know that we are no longer under the Old Covenant, but under a New Covenant, so there are religious practices we do not have to do today to stay in right standing with the Lord. However, God still commissions His people to keep His commands and to obey His Kingdom principles. God tells us that if we do these things, His blessings will be upon our lives.

> *"Call them all together," the Lord instructed, "–men, women, children, and foreigners living among you–to hear the laws of God and to learn his will, so that you will reverence the Lord your God and obey his laws. Do this so that your little children who have not known these laws will hear them and learn how to revere the Lord your God as long as you live in the Promised Land"* (Deut 31:12-13 TLB).

We must understand that there are consequences for not training our children and future generations the things of God and instilling a discipline to follow through with God's principles throughout their lives. Make no mistake about it, for one day we all will stand before the Almighty God and give an account for what we neglected to pass on to future generations.

> *"I am a jealous God, and I will bring the curse of a father's sins upon even the third and fourth generation of the children of those who hate me; but I will show kindness to a thousand generations of those who love me and keep my commandments"* (Deut 5:9b-10 TLB).

Christians must be willing to pull their own weight in the Kingdom to fulfill their responsibilities. When I enlisted in the Air Force, I learned very quick how to pull my own weight. The Air Force teaches its pilots aerial tactics and trains them so they are the best fighter pilots in the world. If these pilots do not practice the principles they learn in their training, they will most likely get themselves or perhaps someone else killed. Our tactic is knowing God's Word which we are to study and live by to defeat our enemy. If you don't know the Word and live it, most likely you, your family, and future generations will suffer for your lack of knowledge and your unwillingness to live by the Bible.

Christians need to fulfill their responsibilities in the Kingdom as did Caleb. When that responsibility is fulfilled and their mission is accomplished they can say like Caleb, "Now give me my mountain." You see, when we are willing to fulfill our responsibility there is grace and power to accomplish our mission no matter how young or old we are. Caleb mentioned this in Joshua chapter fourteen. He was forty years old when Moses used him to spy out the land; then, he still had as much strength at eight-five years old as he did when he was forty.

When we do God's will, which includes training and raising up future generations, there is a ripple effect of blessing that will effect others for years to come. Just as Caleb's children reaped the benefits from their father's obedience, so our children can also reap the rewards of our obedience.

We see in this chapter that when we train and raise up future generations in the things of God's Kingdom, the Lord will restore to His people generational ministry and anointing. However, one area we have neglected to discuss with our children is marriage. The Word says that we are not to be unequally yoked with unbelievers, and it is my opinion that this is one of the biggest reasons that the divorce rate in the church is so high.

Today, I see people who love the Lord and His Kingdom come to church miserable because their spouse cares nothing about the things of God. This, my friend, can be avoided. I will even go a step further and say that when it comes to two Christians being with someone for the rest of their lives, it is important that the two of them be on the same page spiritually, as well.

When I was a single airman in the Air Force I felt a stirring in my spirit that my single days would be over soon, and I began to remember as a young boy my father teaching me that it was important to be praying for my future wife. So, I began to pray for my future wife, and one of the things I would pray is that she would have my same type faith. In other words, I prayed that she would believe in the same things that I believed in as far as spiritual matters are concerned and other things, as well. Not long after I started praying this, God led me to a wonderful church where I met my beautiful wife who is exactly what I prayed for. When you wait on God, He will give you your Isaac instead of an Ishmael, and He will give you the desires of your heart.

I heard a pastor friend give some statistics on how fathers in particular have an influence in their families. If a teenager from an unsaved home, gets born again, there is a 6% chance that the rest of the family will be born again. If a mother from a family of unsaved people gets born again there is a 17% chance that the rest of the family will be born again. In the same type of family where everyone is lost, if a father is born again there is a 95% chance that the rest of the family will get saved. No wonder fathers are under such an attack, from being put down by Jezebel wives on T.V. to struggling with pornography. Fathers, we must rally and allow a revolution to take place in our families. Have a vision, a purpose, and a passion for the things of God within your family.

CHAPTER SEVEN

AFFECTING FUTURE GENERATIONS

I believe today that I am reaping in fields where I have not even sown. Going back just a couple of generations, I know that both sets of my grandparents, as well as my parents, have prayed for their children, grandchildren, and now great-grandchildren and have sown into our lives spiritually, as well as in the natural.

When I was younger, I remember all of my grandparents reading the Bible and talking with me about spiritual things, as well as how to live a godly life. One example of this is every year as the family gathered for Christmas, my grandfather would read the Christmas story to all of his children and grandchildren. As a child I grew tired of hearing this story year after year, after all, I wanted to open my presents; but as I grew up, I began to realize just what my grandfather was doing. He was sowing into his children and reinforcing godly principles in our lives that we will in turn impart to our children. What our grandparents and parents teach us will be their legacy that could live forever through the generations, whether it is good or bad. I do not want to be responsible for future generations living in sin or not having a full life if I sowed bad seed today.

One thing that plagues the world today is racism or a spirit of sectarianism which divides and separates. When children are born, they do not care about other children's race, ethnic origin, or religious affiliation; these things are taught by the parents. In fact, Muslim extremists were not born wanting to be suicide bombers, but were taught and, even in extreme cases, brainwashed to think that it is their call in life to kill and terrorize others.

Children believe what their parents tell them. If a parent tells their child that they are stupid, the child grows up thinking they are stupid. On the other hand, parents who reinforce God's Word in their children's lives with words such as, "You are the head and not the tail. You are fearfully and wonderfully made. Everything that your hand touches will succeed and prosper" will equip their children to tackle any challenge that God has for them instead of fighting through false belief systems that were learned at an early age. Then, instead of saying "I am not able," they will say, "I can do all things through Christ Jesus who strengthens me."

We must be careful and understand the importance of what we sow into the lives of our children. What we teach them now will not only affect them, but will continue to affect future generations. What we sow today will be reaped in future generations.

God wants future generations to go further than previous generations. Philip, the great evangelist who was taken by the Holy Spirit from one region to another instantaneously, had a mighty ministry and taught his children concerning the things of the Lord. In Acts 21:9, we see that Philip had four virgin daughters who prophesied. Philip reproduced himself in his children who ultimately had their own ministry.

David, however, was not a good example of a father; while he taught and trained Solomon in the things of God, David neglected his other children. Absalom, David's own son, tried to form a coup and take over the kingdom that God had ordained for David. Absalom had caused much reproach upon the kingdom. In fact, he was so full of himself, he built a monument to his own glory.

> *During his lifetime Absalom had taken a pillar and erected it in the King's Valley as a monument to himself, for he thought, "I have no son to carry on the memory of my name."*

> *He named the pillar after himself, and it is called Absalom's Monument to this day* (2 Sam 18:18 NIV).

Let us not be like Absalom and try to step into a mantle that God has not called us, but do let us pass on to others the principles of God's Kingdom. When we do this God will give us our own mantle to carry instead of us trying to steal someone else's.

One of the reasons I am writing this book is because I have seen God's blessings upon one generation that are not passed down to the next generation. In fact, the giftings, talents, and anointings at times are not passed down from the previous generation and end up being lost in time.

I have had the privilege of meeting great men and women of God, especially those who have an anointing in the area of music ministry. Those like Pastor Robert Gay, Karen Wheaton, and Eddie James are ones who have reproduced themselves, especially into the lives of younger generations. Just because these great men and women have decided to be obedient to the call that has been placed upon their lives, God has used them mightily in bringing freedom and restoration to upcoming generations. Now, younger generations have been raised up to carry the giftings, talents, and anointings to the generations that follow.

As I said earlier, it has been said that the richest places in the world are cemeteries. Graves and tombs around the world are full of inventions never invented, and books and songs never written. They are full of people who could have achieved great things, but never did. The same can be said about fellow brothers and sisters in Christ who have gone on before us and never used their anointings, talents, or giftings to the extent that God had intended them to be used.

Let us all be good stewards and use what God have given us. When I stand before God's throne, I want Him to say, "Well done good and faithful servant" and be pleased with His son, instead of not using what He has given me and being disobedient and lazy.

> *"Again, it will be like a man going on a journey, who called his servants and entrusted his property to them. To one he gave five talents of money, to another two talents, and to another one talent, each according to his ability. Then he went on his journey. The man who had received the five talents went at once and put his money to work and gained five more. So also, the one with the two talents gained two more. But the man who had received the one talent went off, dug a hole in the ground and hid his master's money.*

"After a long time the master of those servants returned and settled accounts with them. The man who had received the five talents brought the other five. 'Master' he said, 'you entrusted me with five talents. See, I have gained five more.'

"His master replied, 'Well done, good and faithful servant! You have been faithful with a few things; I will put you in charge of many things. Come and share your master's happiness!'

"The man with the two talents also came. 'Master' he said, 'you entrusted me with two talents; see, I have gained two more.'

"His master replied, 'Well done, good and faithful servant! You have been faithful with a few things; I will put you in charge of many things. Come and share your master's happiness!'

"Then the man who had received the one talent came. 'Master' he said, 'I knew that you are a hard man, harvesting where you have not sown and gathering where you have not scattered seed. So I was afraid and went out and hid your talent in the ground. See, here is what belongs to you.'

> *"His master replied, 'You wicked, lazy servant! So you knew that I harvest where I have not sown and gather where I have not scattered seed? Well then, you should have put my money on deposit with the bankers, so that when I returned I would have received it back with interest.*
>
> *"'Take the talent from him and give it to the one who has the ten talents. For everyone who has will be given more, and he will have an abundance. Whoever does not have, even what he has will be taken from him. And throw that worthless servant outside, into the darkness, where there will be weeping and gnashing of teeth'"* (Matt 25:14-30 NIV).

God wants to use us to further His Kingdom. We are to be revolutionists, reformers, up-rooters, people who want to be a part of something bigger than themselves, and people who are instrumental in the ushering in of God's Kingdom. I believe the day of the one-man show is over and that God wants to use all of us in His church for the establishing of His Kingdom. We can achieve this through passing the torch from one generation to another, instead of letting future generations roam in the wilderness trying to figure out what is next.

Generations working together can achieve greater things.

There was a day when God used a few individuals from a generation to bring revelation and restoration to His church, like John Wycliffe, Martin Luther, Charles Parham, William Seymour, and Smith Wigglesworth. We do not have to be a super-Christian for God to use us. Just think, if we reproduce ourselves in others like the Apostle Paul reproduced himself in Timothy, what would things be like today?

When we read the Word, we get a picture in Acts of the early church which is the example of what the New Testament church is to be. Because of a number of things, the church slipped into what we call the Dark Ages or the Great Falling Away. The deterioration of the church covers the period of the Great Falling Away into an apostate condition from the fourth century to the fifteenth century AD. The restoration of the church officially began with the Protestant Movement when God used one man named Martin Luther who had the revelation that the just shall live by faith. This revelation seems simple and elementary to us now, but was a radical concept of its day which brought great persecution. Martin Luther, however, was faithful in the task that God had given him and reproduced himself in others. We can now look back and see how the church has progressed through 500 years of restorational moves of God.

Stop just thinking about yourselves. Churches all across the country take no responsibility for being unproductive; in fact, I hear all the time that the youth of the church are the future and God will use them to do things we are too lazy to do. While the youth of the church are the future generation, this does not excuse the present generation from doing nothing. In fact, I believe this kind of talk actually drives a wedge between the two generations. One looks to the other to accomplish the will of God and, in essence, causes nothing of any substance to be done. God intends for the generations to work together as we discussed earlier in this book, not for one to wish the other would be used to establish the Kingdom.

The church has not been doing its job, and has for the most part been thinking what kind of gushy feeling it can get from today's trend of user-friendly pastors. The church's leadership has been in a popularity contest trying to be liked. However, the pattern we must follow is the one of Jesus who never compromised and seemed to be constantly offending people with God's Word. In fact, He would call the religious leaders of the day a "brood of vipers" and "white washed tombs full of dead men's bones;" try to take up an offering after that message. These churches that will compromise the truth in fear of offending are total failures and have done nothing but keep God's people in an immature state. Remember this: sometimes God will offend the mind to reveal the heart.

Must we be so self-centered and let entire generations that belong in the Kingdom be slain like lambs going to the slaughter? Because of absentee fathers, statistics show that poverty, teen suicide, crime, and teen pregnancy are higher in fatherless homes. We are the richest nation on this planet, and we export more of the Word of God than any other nation. Yet, we have one of the highest suicide rates in the world.

Over the last 30 years, our nation has murdered over 50 million babies through abortion. Over 80 percent of our youth who attend youth groups never return to our churches after they graduate high school. While God has still brought restoration, the church is still failing miserably. I believe God is requiring us to take it to a new level; what was good in the past will not cut it in the future.

When we emulate Jesus and are willing to be pruned and taken through the refiner's fire, everywhere that we go will be transformed. Passing out tracts will no longer cut it, but a demonstration of God in our lives on a daily basis will attract people to the Kingdom. If we do this, things cannot remain the same, and we will change history. God is not looking for another tent revival, but a revolution.

Are we so foolish to think that God needs our marketing strategies to build a successful church? We have pastors in the church today who engage in infidelity and never think about stepping down from ministry. Today compromise of the Word and in ministry is becoming the norm instead of boldly standing up for righteousness. Can it be that those of us who call ourselves friends of the cross are really enemies of it? I encourage you to allow God to do His work within you to be a history changer to the generations.

CHAPTER EIGHT

RAISING UP THE GENERATIONS

As we raise up the generations, we must make a place for them, and in doing so, we must not condemn them when they make a mistake. When you have children you have been given the responsibility by God to raise them up. After all, they are the arrows of the Lord, and your responsibility is to shoot that arrow in order to hit the target. We are to get a vision of our children's abilities, talents, callings, and giftings. Then we are to train them as the Word says, "Train a child in the way he should go, and when he is old he will not depart from it" (Prov 22:6).

When we reproduce ourselves in our children, we take them from sons to men and from men to fathers. What I have had to learn myself is that in order to be a good father, I must first be a good son. When I speak of sons, I am not talking about a specific gender of a child, but about all children.

As true sons, we must be mature and secure enough to acknowledge an individual as a spiritual father and submit to his leadership and to be mentored and trained to become the man God has called us to be. I know many people who are willing to be fathers, but they are not willing to first be sons. In these cases, we see individuals move out prematurely into a mantle that has not yet been passed to them and therefore, become illegitimate sons who go on to reproduce more illegitimate children.

We must train our children. There is no "big" Holy Spirit and "little" Holy Spirit, but just the Holy Spirit. We can be rest assured that no age is too young to start training in the things of God. Even when my daughter was a newborn, my wife and I had her in church and did not just bring her and leave her in the nursery, but brought her into the worship services and taught her to worship God. There are times I look around and see other children just sitting in their seats coloring or playing with toys, but I have made a decision that while in God's House it is imperative that my child learns the importance of worshiping the Lord. You might think this is extreme but God takes this very seriously, and I am the one that He will hold accountable for what I teach or do not teach my children.

I had a conversation with an individual about his child who was actually a young adult, and this young lady had informed the father that she had felt God calling her to another state and had a particular call upon her life. This gentleman informed me that God does not need His people to go to certain places to do His will, and they can basically just be free in Jesus and do His will wherever they may roam. As the man continued, he said that if God ever were to tell His people anything it would be confirmed after months of prayer and fasting. This sounds just dandy, and there are times that we must spend time in fasting and prayer; however, this theology has no biblical foundation. In fact, we must go back to the Word and we will see David praising and worshiping God in the fields with his sheep. But as we all know the story, God had a plan for David somewhere else which was the battlefield where he slew Goliath that would propel him into his destiny as king.

Another point I would like to make is that we must not be so prideful to think that God cannot speak to our children directly. The Bible is full of God speaking to His people immediately after seeking Him. Again, David, when he came to Ziklag, found that the Amalekites had taken his wives and children captive, so David called upon the Lord and the Lord responded.

> *So David inquired of the LORD, saying, "Shall I pursue this troop? Shall I overtake them?" And He answered him, "Pursue, for you shall surely overtake them and without fail recover all"* (1 Sam 30:8).

Train up your children, get them involved, and teach them to worship the Lord and to seek His face with everything within them all the days of their lives. Many Christians do not get involved in church until adulthood. Find out what your children are good at and enjoy, and get them plugged in. A father will see a child's giftings, talents, and anointings and help them develop, use, and become comfortable with them in order to become the person God has called them to be.

> *Now no chastening seems to be joyful for the present, but painful; nevertheless, afterward it yields the peaceable fruit of righteousness to those who have been trained by it* (Heb 12:11).

As we train our children, we need to encourage them to use their gifts. This process can at times seem frustrating, but in the end we will see them bear much fruit instead of just being fruity. There is nothing more rewarding than seeing your child develop and become a good steward of their giftings, talents, and anointings.

I know a lot of parents who do not seek to understand their children; they are so out of touch they cannot even relate on any level. As I was growing up, computers began to be a part of every home in America so the children in these homes grew up using computers on a daily basis. In fact, the school system had computers in classes, even in the elementary schools. A large portion of adults, however, were intimidated by this machine and refused to even find out how it worked and how it could make things more convenient for them. So they just left it up to their children to learn, and this being the case, sometimes the children learned incorrectly. The same is true today with the older generation in the church; they know God will do great things, but they leave it up to the younger generation to figure it out.

God brings restoration to His church, not limited to a certain age group, but through a generation of people of the same like-mindedness who are willing to usher in the things of the Kingdom. As we discussed earlier in this book, I do not know how many times I have heard in the churches across America that God will bring revival and His next great move through the youth. However, every year when the senior youth graduate high school, eighty percent of them never even return to the church. Now, I am not saying that God does not use the youth in a powerful way, or that He cannot use them for revival and further His

Kingdom. I have seen God do great and mighty things with the youth that I have not seen Him do with others. We must have a bigger picture than what we have had, and regardless of age, we cannot just leave it up to the youth to figure out. We need to be a generation of like-minded believers and not continue to enforce the generation gaps. We should not be lazy and leave it up to the youth to do God's will without training and mentoring them.

When you encourage and exhort you empower people to succeed. Those whom I have allowed to speak into my life have encouraged me, and in doing so, have kept me from giving up on challenging situations. In return, they have empowered me to succeed and overcome. You see, we are always supposed to be overcomers and never the victim.

There is a real war going on, but we are never supposed to lose this war. If you are living a defeated existence, get around people who will encourage and exhort you, and receive it. I know people who say they want encouragement, but in reality, they reject the encouragement and want you to throw a pity party with them. One word of warning, choose wisely with whom you fellowship and don't get trapped into participating in any pity parties, because in doing so you are literally empowering others to fail and enabling them to remain in their defeated world.

CHAPTER NINE

FACING THE GIANTS

Then David said to the Philistine, "You come to me with a sword, with a spear, and with a javelin. But I come to you in the name of the LORD of hosts, the God of the armies of Israel, whom you have defied. This day the LORD will deliver you into my hand, and I will strike you and take your head from you. And this day I will give the carcasses of the camp of the Philistines to the birds of the air and the wild beasts of the earth, that all the earth may know that there is a God in Israel" (1 Sam 17:45-46).

Be willing to face the giants. When people get saved most of the time they do not really realize that they have just enlisted into the real army of God, and in this army, there are giants to slay. Theses giants can sometimes be generational issues that have been passed down your family line. They can also be issues like failure, addiction, depression, accident proneness, or living a defeated life, among other things. We must be willing to face these giants and defeat them so that our children do not have to. As my wife and I have looked back over our family lines, we have noticed issues that were passed down, sometimes every other generation if not generation after generation. Instead of being generational blessings, these were generational curses that negatively affected members of our families. This does not mean that these family members are bad people, it just means that they were handed a bad bill of goods from somewhere up the family line.

My wife and I decided that no matter how ugly these issues got we had to deal with them–eradicate them out of our lives–so we do not pass them on to our children and continue this vicious cycle. Let me tell you, it has not been easy all the time. In fact, when you go out onto the battlefield to face your Goliath, sometimes you feel like you are the only one out there. However, God can give you boldness and grace to empower you to slay these giants. There are no wimps in God's army so be as bold as David was when he faced his giant and say, "Today, giant, you're going down." When the giants come telling you how small you are, just remind him how big your God is!

Get a long-range vision–that's how God sees things. Do not limit Him by just thinking only about today. What if great men and women of the past raised up others to carry on their ministry, like Smith Wigglesworth, John G. Lake, Kathryn Kuhlman, or Aimee Semple McPherson, in order to carry on the ministry like Elijah did with Elisha? I have to think to myself, what would this world be like?

It is sad to see people of God, especially ministers, who have powerful ministries and do not pass on their anointings, giftings, knowledge, and points of view to others that are around them. After all, the world has no problem giving its point of view.

Be patient with God's process. We are a microwave generation and are used to having it our way at Burger King®. God's way of doing things is different than our way. If we are not patient with God's process and do not pass the test the first time, He will require us to go around the mountain again. I do not know about you, but I do not want to go through the hassle of having to waste time going through the process again when I could have gotten it right the first time.

The military at times drops paratroopers onto a particular drop zone; however, if the plane misses the mark, it has to circle back around and drop its paratroopers in the correct place. The same thing goes for bombers dropping bombs. You do not want to drop your troops in the wrong place, scattered around the countryside where they will be ineffective. You also don't want bombs falling on schools, hospitals, and civilian targets. So the military goes to great extents to train and obey orders so they will hit the mark every time.

When we are patient with the process that God takes us through we will hit the mark at the right place at the right time. Let me say that it really is just easier when we are patient and trust the Lord in every situation we go through. You might think this statement is easier said than done. However, when you hand over your situation or process to the Lord and truly leave it with Him instead of picking it back up again worrying, fretting, and getting impatient about it, then it really is easier. Then you are not wasting so much of your life fighting the process God has for you.

When you understand that God's process is always the best way, life gets much easier by going with His flow instead of resisting and fighting against it. I see Christians living a defeated or worrisome life because they want to do things their way. They have trouble believing and trusting God for small things like paying their bills, healing, or restoring strained relationships when they have no problem trusting Him to forgive their sin and cleanse them from all unrighteousness. Get with the program and just trust God and be patient with the process that He takes you through.

Creating a new lineage is what we do when we reproduce ourselves in our children or become fathers to the fatherless. Think of all the future generations that will be affected who are not even born yet. We can have the same attitude of our ancestors who would say, "We never did it that way before," or we can dare to step out in faith and change the world. We create a new lineage by being more concerned about what God wants done, instead of being concerned about what some relative might think.

CHAPTER TEN

TRAINING YOUR CHILDREN

God has not called us or our children to live in defeat, but to live consistently in a state of victory. We are never supposed to lose against the enemy. Now, I am not saying the devil will never attack you, but if you or your children are getting beat up on a daily basis or living a defeated existence something is wrong. We must be an example to our kids and demonstrate that we will not put up with the enemy living in our homes. We can teach our children not to be cocky, but confident in God so they can trust Him and have an expectation of God's best.

Our children learn what we demonstrate to them. If we demonstrate fear, doubt, defeat, rejection, and unforgiveness, they will govern their lives by these things. If we demonstrate faith, trust in the Lord, and belief in the entire uncompromised Word of God, then we will raise up champions for God's Kingdom.

As I said, we are never supposed to lose this thing; in fact, the devil needs to dread every morning we wake up! Seriously, if the enemy is not threatened by us then we are doing something wrong. In addition, since we are supposed to consistently live in a state of victory, then how are we going to teach and demonstrate to others how we are to live? I know Christians who love telling people that they go to church or that they are Christians. However, they speak with filthy language, live an undisciplined life, walk by their emotions, and steal from their employer or employees.

As people of God, we are expected to live our lives in victory, but also with stability. Think about it–if you are a nonbeliever being witnessed to by a Christian whose life is a mess, then why would you even want to be a Christian? This principle not only goes for ministers of the Word, but also the everyday believer.

Remember this, God is more interested in a person's character than their ministry. If you live in defeat and you have character issues like those that we discussed earlier, ask the Holy Spirit to reveal it to you, and ask Him to deliver you from whatever you might need. If you do not let God deal with your issues, then your issues will deal with you, and you end up being a reproach to God's Kingdom. You might think this is harsh language, but I know ministers of the gospel who operate immorally in the area of finances. I know of others who have committed adultery and never even gave thought to stepping down from ministry in order to deal with their issues. These people, full-time ministers or your everyday believer, turn people away from God and end up being a reproach to God's Kingdom.

> *For we do not wrestle against flesh and blood, but against principalities, against powers, against the rulers of the darkness of this age, against spiritual hosts of wickedness in the heavenly places* (Eph 6:12).

Wage vengeance upon the kingdoms of darkness. This is a call to arms. God is raising up an army, and this army is dressed for battle. All the religious talk we have heard throughout the years about how Christians should just be peaceful and suffer through the attacks of the enemy is nothing but garbage. God's people traditionally love to fight! Christians should love to wage vengeance upon the enemy because that is a part of who we are.

When we were children, we all admired the fastest runner, big league ball players, and toughest boxers. Even so, Christians love a winner and should not tolerate a loser. The loser I am referring to is the enemy that Jesus fought against and won.

You see, the devil was not put here to torment us, but he was put here so that we could torment him. We already fight from a position of victory. Far too often, the roles have been reversed and Christians think that it is the devil's job to do the tormenting. However, he will if we give him the chance, but it is truly our job to exercise God's judgment upon the enemy. One thing we should realize is that satan only has as much power as we give him.

> *For though we walk in the flesh, we do not war according to the flesh. For the weapons of our warfare are not carnal but mighty in God for pulling down strongholds* (2 Cor 10:3-4).

God's people that know who they are in Christ fight to win every time because the very thought of losing is hateful to the Christian. The body of Christ is a team that lives, eats, and sleeps as a team; therefore, illustrating to us the importance of just showing up for practice because when we don't go to church the whole team suffers. This humanistic individuality talk we hear from the secular society is a bunch of garbage. The people who write this stuff about individuality don't know anything about real battle and what it takes to win a supernatural war. Therefore, they live a defeated existence–torn apart by the enemy. The devil doesn't just eat unbelievers for lunch, he also preys upon believers who are unaware of who they are in God's Kingdom.

"Beat your plowshares into swords, And your pruning hooks into spears;" (Joel 3:10).

I believe that the most dangerous position to be in is that of a lukewarm Christian. The enemy does not have to waste his time with the unbeliever because the unbeliever is living a wasted, non-threatening life. When the on-fire, Spirit-filled Christian sees the work of the enemy he goes after him and tears him to shreds. The lukewarm Christian knows just enough to be saved, but not enough to fight off or even defeat the enemy, and therefore, has a big red target on his back. This is one reason to be planted in a good church full of life instead of a dead, dry, religious church where no one knows who they are in Christ and what they should be doing for His kingdom; when these people leave church, they go back to their defeated lives.

"From the lips of children and infants you have ordained praise because of your enemies, to silence the foe and the avenger" (Ps 8:2 NIV).

Now we, on the other hand, have the best weapons to fight in the war of the ages. We have the gifts of the Spirit, the five-fold ministry, praise, and prayer which are among many weapons that are in our arsenal. You know, I almost would say that I pity the enemy, but not really, because the devil does not have a chance when it comes to God's people raising the flag of battle. I can hear satan now, "Oh no, they're awake again!" We are not going to play patty-cake with the enemy, but we are going to rip him to shreds; we are going to destroy principalities and powers by the bushel. To many Christians, this kind of talk is foreign. In fact, one brother in the Lord was disturbed by this talk and was afraid I would stir the devil up and get him mad at me. He said, "Oh Brother Shane, you don't need to talk about the devil that way. After all, he is more powerful than you are!" I stood there and felt a chuckle in my spirit and I said to him, "No, he isn't, for greater is He who is in me than he that is in the world!"

You see a person's true character when the pressure is on. Some Christians don't know what they will do when things come down to the wire. But, I say when you look over and see how the devil has destroyed the lives of your loved ones, you will know what to do. You take the fight to him and so should every Christian until he finally realizes that every time he messes with one of God's people there is a price to pay.

We are not merely holding on, we are possessing. I hear some Christians say, "Well, I am just holding on." As God's people, we have been commissioned not to just hold on, but to retake ground the enemy has stolen from us. We do not hold on and let the enemy do that! We advance constantly and are not interested in holding on to anything except the enemy when he comes around. We are going to hold on to him by the neck and kick him in the teeth. When I am an old man and my grandchildren are on my knee and they ask me what I did in the greatest battle of good versus evil, I won't have to say that I got my rear-end kicked by the hordes of hell.

Take authority over satan. When you stand as a representative of God's Kingdom in the name of Jesus, the enemy has to submit. Satan should not have authority over us; it is the born-again, Spirit-filled believers who have authority over the devil. True leaders will stand up to the threats of the enemy. God's people need to get the revelation that it is the church that has been given the assignment of punishing the enemy for his rebellion against God. Then, we will see greater revival and revelation released than the church has ever seen before.

Be a true leader. You can be a true leader without being a tyrant. Being a leader sometimes requires you to go into uncharted territory as a pioneer or a forerunner, when others want to stay in their comfort zones. A father, either spiritual or natural, is a leader, and as a leader, you are called upon to exhibit strength under pressure.

I was with a friend on his boat one day and the waves and wind were so powerful they almost ran us aground. However, we quickly let out the anchors and when they gripped the ocean floor they provided the stability we needed. It made me think of leaders and how they are anchors to the people around them. Many leaders find themselves in situations where people come to them for encouragement, advice, and prayer because the leader provides stability and strength in the midst of turmoil.

Your pastor should be this type of leader, one who truly leads. The pastor of the church where I attend is one such leader. In fact, I do not know anyone with more integrity who is willing to do what God has called him to do, no matter if it harelips the devil and the entire world. He leads with stability that comforts, encourages, and gives direction in the midst of the storm.

Jesus was the ultimate leader, a leader who set His face like flint to go into the city that would have Him crucified. He was such a leader that people would, in return, lay their lives down for Him. In fact, many still do to this day.

"Death and life are in the power of the tongue, And those who love it will eat its fruit" (Prov 18:21).

The Bible says plenty about the words that we speak. We can speak life or death over something by the words that we say. Speak words of life over your children. I hear parents all the time speaking curses over their kids. People do not realize the power their words have over their children. If parents tell their children that they are unable to do something, then the child grows up thinking they are unable. The words that you speak over your children have the power to inhibit or propel that child, so it is important to speak words that will cause them to be a success in whatever endeavors they encounter.

I was talking to a parent one day who was telling me about all the trouble their child has caused them and how this child gets violent, speaks with filthy language, and lies. Now, what this parent will not tell you is that the behavior this child exhibits (which I have seen on numerous occasions) is the same behavior the parent uses. You cannot puff on a cigarette and expect your children not to do the same. It is ironic how people live an undisciplined life, and they wonder why their children are doing the same thing they themselves are guilty of doing. Parents like these make more excuses about why their child cannot do something instead of speaking God's Word over them and encouraging their child to excel.

I am not trying to puff myself up; after all, I will be the first one to tell you I have made my share of mistakes. However, I speak God's Word over my children like, "You are the righteousness of God in Christ Jesus," "You are the head and not the tail," "You can do all things through Christ who gives you strength," and "God has not given you a spirit of fear but one of power, love, and a sound mind." These are just a few of what my wife and I speak over our children. What you speak over your child is the foundation of who they become and it will either propel or hinder them throughout their life's journey. Ask yourself, "What kind of fruit do I want to see in my children?"

CHAPTER ELEVEN

WHAT IF YOU DON'T HAVE CHILDREN?

If you do not have children, you can still be that father-type figure that raises others up in the Kingdom. In the first chapter of first Samuel, we see Eli taking Samuel as a boy into the house of the Lord and raising him up to serve in God's Kingdom.

God will bring those He wants you to mentor. God will bring people across your path that need the very things that He has placed within you. You can be an example to those who have not had a good role model in their lives and show them what it means to be a godly person. We are to be reproducers of re-producers which means that we are to mentor others in the things that God has taught us. The world is reproducing itself in ungodly ways every day; God wants us to reproduce in His people His principles and ways of doing things.

Paul refers to Timothy as his son in the faith to whom he imparted things. Timothy was not Paul's natural son, but was a son in a spiritual sense. There have been those who have taken the whole subject of spiritual fathers and spiritual children into a place of error, but that does not mean we throw the baby out with the bath water.

Those who are like spiritual fathers to you (like your pastor) are not to replace our natural fathers, but to be that person that mentors us in the things of God or one that we allow to speak wisdom into our lives if your natural father is not able to. Paul did not replace Timothy's natural father, but was able to help usher him into the anointing and mantle God had for him.

Another example of a spiritual father is Elijah to Elisha. At first, Elisha was one who had a servant's heart who was just willing to serve the man of God. However, as Elisha served Elijah he, through his service and being with Elijah on a daily basis, was given a double-portion anointing. You, too, can mentor and raise up others to pass on generational anointings, like Elijah did with Elisha.

God is replacing generational curses with generational blessings. A young lady that I know was having trouble not wanting to forgive her mother for things that most people would find minuscule; however, these things were a big deal to her. I looked at the big picture and saw that the parents have almost the exact same views toward one of their mothers. I remembered a conversation I had with the grandmother in this family, and she was telling me of very similar situations of family disunity throughout two previous generations. Family disunity has tormented this family for at least four generations. What this family must do is see what is really going on–that this is a generational curse that must be dealt with so it is not passed down to yet another generation. We have to call it what it is and say the curse stops and generational blessing start with us.

The parents of this young lady need to see that they themselves have not demonstrated God's forgiveness, and their daughter is just doing what has been demonstrated all these years. But there is good news! God is a God of restoration, and it is His best when families operate in unity instead of letting the enemy bring offense and ultimately division within relationships. So swallow your pride and do what is right, and God will meet you halfway. He will exchange your generational curse for a generational blessing.

CHAPTER TWELVE

THE BLESSING OF ABRAHAM

The blessing of Abraham, found in Deuteronomy 28, is a generational blessing that will be passed down to my seed. The Word of God works every time someone puts it into effect. Just like natural physical laws that we use every day, spiritual laws work when they are put into effect. Some of these laws are the laws of sowing and reaping and the law of blessing and cursing.

We see a great example of the laws of blessing and cursing. If you obey God's Word the result will be blessing upon you and your family; if you do not obey God's Word then curses will be the result. I often think of it like this: if you are obedient to God's Word then you will be under God's canopy of protection and blessing. However, if you are disobedient to God's Word, there are consequences if you step outside His canopy that bring protection and blessing into a place where you are exposed to whatever elements the enemy is raining down.

Nevertheless, here we see in the book of Deuteronomy that God also punishes those who operate in disobedience.

During this time of disobedience, many immature Christians even start to blame God for the bad results they are experiencing; however, it is a direct result of their disobedience to God's Word. For example, God's Word says to tithe, and if we do not obey we are robbing God and are cursed with a curse. Even in the New Testament Jesus says that we are to tithe. But I know Christians who refuse to be faithful to God's Word to tithe, and they might see a little blessing here and there but more often they just don't know why they are always in debt, their children are constantly in the emergency room, their belongings deteriorate and break down, their marriages are falling apart, and there is no peace in their home. Then, I see people who live a controlled and disciplined life who live in obedience and tithe, so their dollar goes further, their children are healthy and happy, and there is peace in the home. It is just easier to do things God's way. Besides, for everything He has done for me, obedience is the least I can do for Him. When we are obedient to God we live under the blessings of Abraham, and the blessings not only affect us, but future generations, as well.

The decisions you make today will affect future generations. I was in a meeting with

Pastor Robert Gay one morning and he told me something I will never forget: when we are confronted with a decision to make, we can make either the right decision that will bring blessing, or we can choose to make the wrong decision which will bring consequences.

One such example is found in Joshua chapter seven. Achan had been disobedient to the Lord's instructions and his whole family paid the price. You can bring blessing into your home or curses into your home. You can play praise and worship music in your house and keep your television on God TV, but at the same time if you are having an extra-marital affair be assured it will bring a curse into your home. You can use your hands to bless your children when they go to bed at night, but if you turn around and embrace another lover other than your wife, you bring not blessing anymore, but judgment upon yourselves. You can be anointed to minister the Word of the Lord, but if you are not tithing, the Word says that you are even stealing from the hand of God, and you are cursed with a curse. God will not stand for His people to bring reproach upon His Kingdom by using their giftings in the church and doing ungodly things in secret. Whatever ungodly things you do in secret, God will eventually expose openly. I know of many powerful ministries that took decades to build and were brought down in one day because of secret sins.

Not that making the right decision is always easy, but we need to realize that the decisions we make affect more people than just us. They can even affect generations to come. There have been powerful ministers of the gospel who have affected literally millions of people that when they were still in the womb their mother was presented with a choice, the choice to give birth or to abort the pregnancy. Yet, I think of what the world would be like if these ministers were never born to bring blessing, freedom, deliverance, and salvation to the people of the world.

Do not just make flippant decisions, but base the decisions you make according to the Word of God and see the blessing it brings, not only to you, but to others, too.

"Those who are planted in the house of the LORD shall flourish in the courts of our God" (Ps 92:13).

Make God's Kingdom a priority. Now this is a touchy subject, especially here in the United States. Christians are faithful people; they will be at work on time, school on time, they will not miss soccer practice or P.T.A. meetings. They will even be faithful to keep their lawn manicured, but they just cannot be faithful to go to church. They say that they are faithful when they go to church twice a month, but come on, that is not really being faithful.

Going to church every time the doors are open does not make you saved either, and I realize that some people go because they think that church is a spiritual slot machine and maybe they will just get lucky. However, I go on a regular weekly basis because the Bible says that we are to go there, give there, and eat there. If we are not at church on a regular basis our spiritual diet is incomplete because we miss too many meals and are unhealthy, weak Christians.

I go to church as much as I do because it keeps me grounded, encouraged, and edified. The Word says that faith comes by hearing the Word of God. When I hear my pastor preach the Word, my faith is increased. The Lord even speaks to me and gives me revelation in the midst of a sermon or even challenges me to become a better Christian.

> *For as the body is one and has many members, but all the members of that one body, being many, are one body, so also is Christ. For by one Spirit we were all baptized into one body–whether Jews or Greeks, whether slaves or free–and have all been made to drink into one Spirit. For in fact the body is not one member but many. If the foot should say, "Because I am not a hand, I am not of the body," is it therefore not of the body? And if the*

ear should say, "Because I am not an eye, I am not of the body," is it therefore not of the body? If the whole body were an eye, where would be the hearing? If the whole were hearing, where would be the smelling? But now God has set the members, each one of them, in the body just as He pleased. And if they were all one member, where would the body be? But now indeed there are many members, yet one body. And the eye cannot say to the hand, "I have no need of you"; nor again the head to the feet, "I have no need of you." No, much rather, those members of the body which seem to be weaker are necessary. And those members of the body which we think to be less honorable, on these we bestow greater honor; and our unpresentable parts have greater modesty, but our presentable parts have no need. But God composed the body, having given greater honor to that part which lacks it, that there should be no schism in the body, but that the members should have the same care for one another. And if one member suffers, all the members suffer with it; or if one member is honored, all the members rejoice with it. Now you are the body of Christ, and members individually. And God has appointed these

> *in the church: first apostles, second prophets, third teachers, after that miracles, then gifts of healings, helps, administrations, varieties of tongues. Are all apostles? Are all prophets? Are all teachers? Are all workers of miracles? Do all have gifts of healings? Do all speak with tongues? Do all interpret? But earnestly desire the best gifts. And yet I show you a more excellent way* (1 Cor 12:12-31).

I am part of the body of Christ, and I need my brothers and sisters in the Lord. I need their giftings, talents, and anointings, and they need mine, as well. I cannot say that I have no need for them. If I do, I become an unhealthy Christian being cut off from the rest of the body. If someone cuts off their finger, that finger will ultimately die if it is not reattached. The same goes for Christians who do not go to church. Either they die spiritually, or they become spiritual flakes having no stability being tossed to and fro by the storms of life. Besides, everything being said, just being in God's house and around like-minded believers is the least I can do for Him.

CHAPTER THIRTEEN

THERE IS A REASON TO INVEST IN THE FUTURE OF YOUR CHILDREN

The things you cherish the most you will spend time on. My wife and I will spend time with our children because we cherish them. We take trips to the park, read to them, and get on the floor to play. We do all this because we want to invest in our daughters, and the byproduct of this is fun and great joy.

If you cherish that cherry red Corvette in your garage, I guarantee you'll spend time washing, waxing, and tinkering around on it, or for you it might be that boat you enjoy taking out on a pretty day. Regardless of what it is, you spend time on what you cherish. The same should go for our children. However, I see a lot of parents who have their priorities mixed up and would rather do anything than to spend time with their children–mentoring, loving, teaching, and just enjoying the beautiful gifts that God gave them.

My wife and I took our first daughter to the park one day and I noticed a child wanting her dad to spend time paying attention to her. But you could tell having to spend time with his child was a chore, and it saddened me to see this little girl wanting to have some daddy time and Daddy was not going for that.

Many times, people view God the same way they see their own fathers, either good or bad. If their father never kept their word then they will grow up seeing God as One who will not keep His Word either. If their father never had time for them, they will see God as One who does not have time for them either. Furthermore, if their father is a tyrant, then they will see God as a tyrant. It is important to have our lives in order and our priorities straight because how you conduct your family effects more than just you.

Our children are the future and if we do not train them in the things of God, the world will train them in the things of the world. In this day and age, our children are being bombarded everyday with the ungodliness that the world has to offer. I know a lot of parents who let the television be their child's babysitter. Many homes across America have TVs in every bedroom, and while a TV or computer is not necessarily a bad thing, it can be if it is not properly monitored by the parents. The fact of the matter is we have to be the ones that influence our children and not allow forms of entertainment or friends to take our place.

Like I have said before, it is not the church or the youth pastor's responsibility to instill spiritual principles in your child; it is the parent's responsibility. The church and the pastors should just be reinforcing what the parents have already deposited within their own children.

I know Christian youth who are on their computers until one and two o'clock in the morning putting inappropriate pictures and comments on their My Space®, Facebook®, or Twitter®. Some are even sneaking out of the house and meeting up with the opposite sex, getting drunk or high, and their Christian parents do not even have a clue or maybe they do not want to know. I am exposing this because it is becoming a reproach to the Kingdom of God and these things ought not be! If parents keep living in denial, their children will end up being casualties in a battle that could have been prevented.

"A good man leaves an inheritance to his children's children, But the wealth of the sinner is stored up for the righteous" (Prov 13:22).

Pass on more than a financial inheritance, but a spiritual inheritance, too. The

Bible says that a good man will leave an inheritance to his children's children. Most of the time we think of just leaving a financial inheritance; however, we need to think of leaving a spiritual inheritance for them, as well. I am writing this book to leave a spiritual inheritance for future generations.

There are more natural things that are passed down the lineage than spiritual things. We need to see the importance of passing down a spiritual heritage to other generations. For example, teaching the younger generations the revelations that God has shown you, how to live a godly life, how to stand up for godly principles, and not compromise.

I was watching a well-known pastor on TV one day and the interviewer asked this pastor basically if homosexuality was wrong, and this pastor's response was, "Well, I just don't go there." I will tell you what my response was: "What do you mean you don't go there?" As a pastor and even as a Christian, we have a responsibility to stand for righteousness and boldly proclaim what God's Word says, and this minister's response is "I don't go there?" I tell you, if I could have reached through that TV screen, I would have. We cannot teach our children to compromise and accept ungodly things. We need to pass down a heritage that is based on godly principles with no compromising because of the fear of man.

Don't just exist, but make a difference. There is a large portion of Christians who really do not make a difference in God's Kingdom. God wants you to make a difference in this world and not just exist and get by, but to impact the lives of those around you. Making a difference in someone's life in the natural is a good thing, like giving to the poor or encouraging someone who is down, but sometimes we neglect to think of sowing into a person's life spiritually.

The church has become so watered down because these spiritual principles were not passed down through the years and the upcoming generations are now starting user-friendly churches and think the important things in the church should be another program or event. While there is nothing wrong with programs or events, the Word is watered down, the Holy Spirit is left out of the picture, there is a fear to preach some things that might offend somebody, and so the important things are left untaught and undone. These churches and pastors are nothing but hirelings and prostitutes; they compromise the Word and deny the power of Almighty God. What we need is to get back to basics and say, "Lord, start with me; make me into the person you have truly called me to be. Let me be a mouthpiece to the generations to proclaim your goodness, mercy, and grace."

God is always doing something new. If we are not moving forward with God, then we are backsliding and being left in the dust when the rest of the army is advancing the Kingdom. You can tell real quick who the Kingdom people are and those who are just dead-weight trying to keep out of hell.

Be willing to be a Kingdom person and stand for righteousness and teach others to do the same; you will set the course for future generations. All that is necessary for the triumph of evil is for good men do nothing, so I refuse to stand by and do nothing any longer. When God's people understand His pattern for their family, it will change the world!

ABOUT THE AUTHOR

SHANE HUSEBY and his wife, Julia, are healing and deliverance ministers at High Praise Worship Center under the leadership of Pastor Robert Gay in Panama City, Florida. His varied background in business and ministry provides unique insight into developing godly leaders within the home and taking back what the enemy has stolen.

Drawing upon Scripture and his own personal experiences in family and ministry, Shane sheds light on the Kingdom example men are to be within their homes and to others within their sphere of influence. Leaning upon God's Word and His wisdom, you will be encouraged and motivated to reproduce Kingdom principles within the younger generations.

Parsons Publishing House

Your Voice Your World™

SILENCING THE ENEMY WITH PRAISE
by Pastor Robert Gay

In this book, you will learn what God's Word says about the power of praise to: destroy the strongholds of Satan; bring healing, deliverance, and restoration; release the prophetic word; win the victory in spiritual warfare; and drive out demonic principalities. $11.95.

70 REASONS FOR SPEAKING IN TONGUES
by Dr. Bill Hamon

Over 600 million Christians have received the Holy Spirit gift of tongues, and 95% of Spirit-baptized Christians only utilize 10% of the benefits of speaking in tongues. Learn how to use your spirit language to activate more faith and increase God's love and power within your life and ministry (216 pages). $14.95.

Available at your local bookstore.
www.ParsonsPublishingHouse.com